LIONA BOYD

A Guitar for Christmas

Une guitare pour Noël

Eine Gitarre für Weihnachten

A classical guitar folio for the best-selling
CBS Master Works album FM 37248.
Cover photo by Deborah Tuberville.

CONTENTS

HAL•LEONARD® CORPORATION

7777 W. BLUEMOUND RD. P.O. BOX 13819 MILWAUKEE, WI 53213

LIONA BOYD

Photo: James Loewen

At Christmas time when Liona Boyd was 14 years old, her parents gave her a guitar that they had brought back from Spain. It changed the course of her life, and Liona is now recognized all over the world as "The First Lady of the Guitar."

Through her extensive international concert tours, television shows and 13 best selling records, Liona Boyd has brought her guitar to both classical and popular audiences.

There are no more familiar songs than those associated with Christmas, and Liona's Christmas album on CBS reached platinum sales. Here is a selection of those guitar arrangements plus many other seasonal favorites.

Richard Fortin was born in Québec and studied at L'Ecole Supérieure de Musique de Nicolet and at the University of Montreal. In 1983 he moved to Toronto and began to compose and arrange for guitar. He has written many original works for Liona Boyd which she often includes in her concert programs. Richard has co-written a guitar concerto with Liona and performed on her new CBS recording "Persona."

SILENT NIGHT

DECK THE HALLS

I SAW THREE SHIPS

O COME ALL YE FAITHFUL

Maestoso

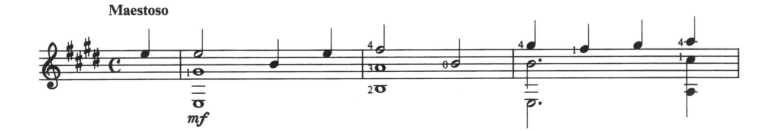

TOY SOLDIERS

Arranged by Eric Robertson
for Liona Boyd

ANGELS WE HAVE HEARD ON HIGH

WE THREE KINGS

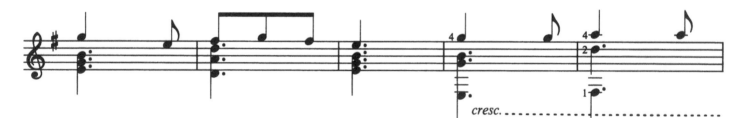

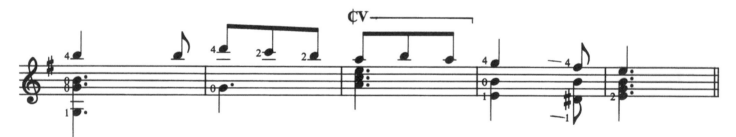

mf

cresc.

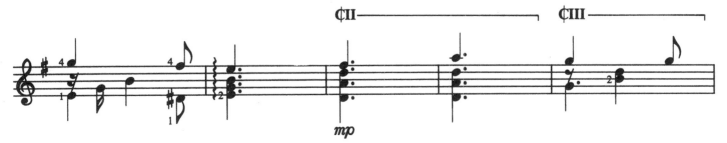

CII ——————— CIII ———————

mp

CIII ———————

CV ———————

rall. e dim.

O CHRISTMAS TREE

Nobile

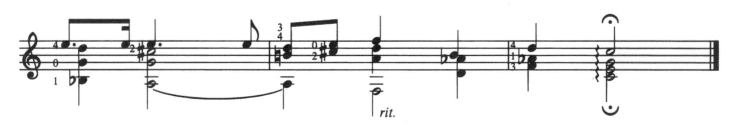

JOY TO THE WORLD

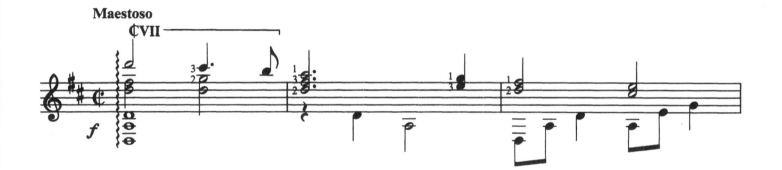

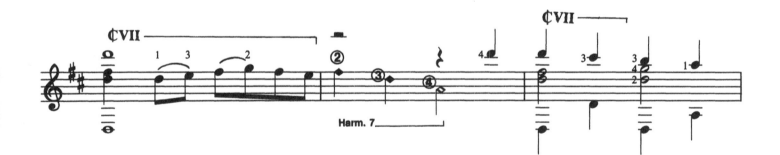

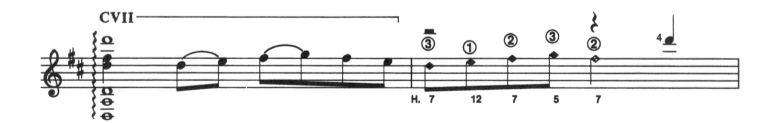

16

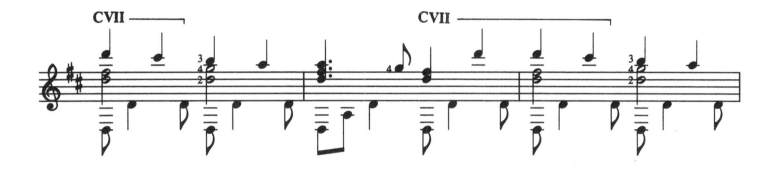

O LITTLE TOWN OF BETHLEHEM

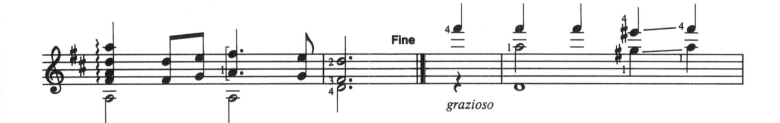

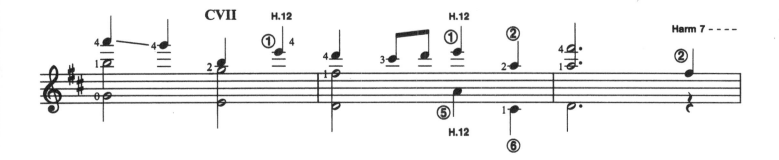

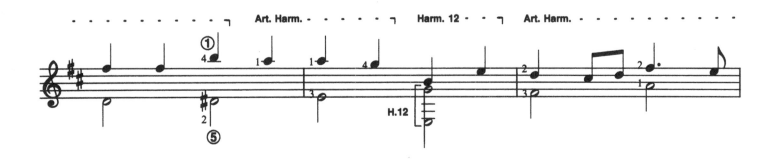

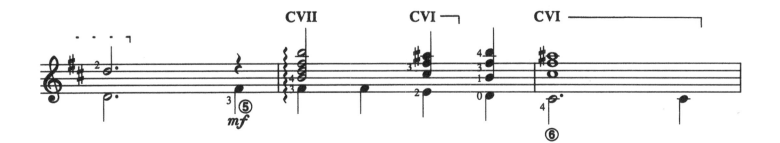

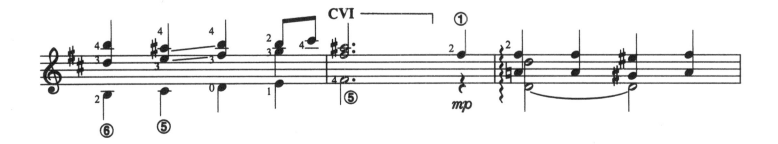

ONCE IN ROYAL DAVID'S CITY

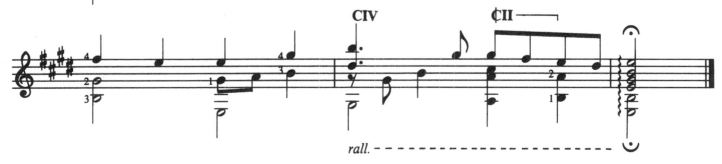

GOD REST YE MERRY, GENTLEMEN

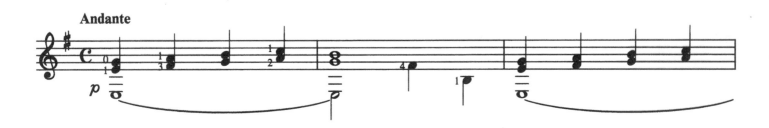

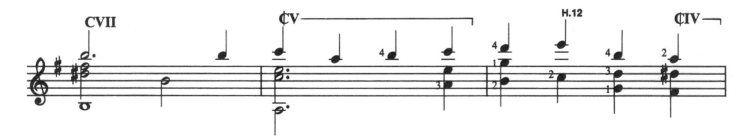

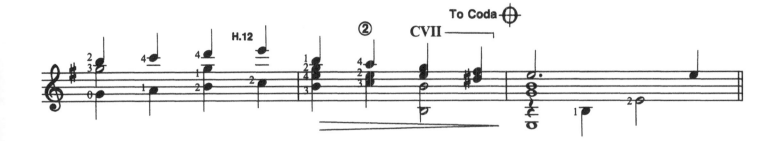

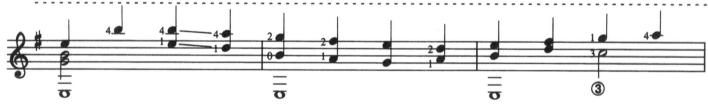

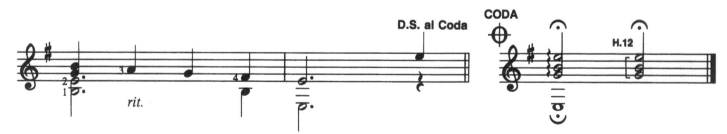

DECK THE HALLS

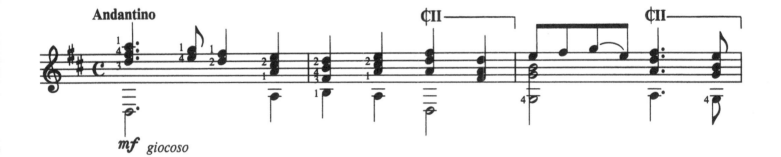

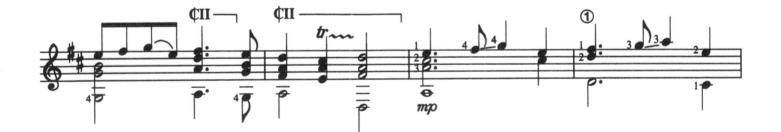

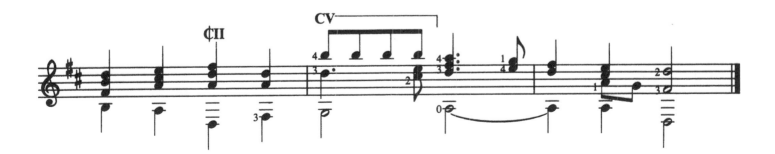

I SAW THREE SHIPS

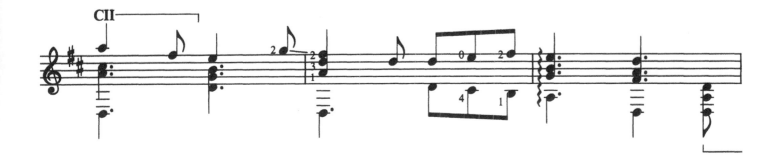

Tambora

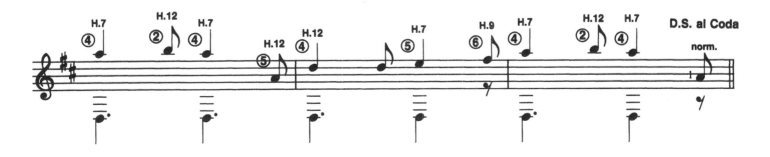

D.S. al Coda

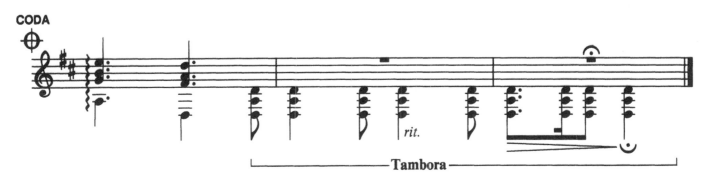

CODA

Tambora

HARK! THE HERALD ANGELS SING/
IL EST NE LE DIVIN ENFANT

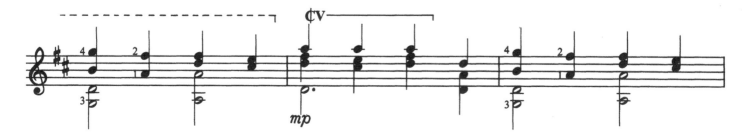

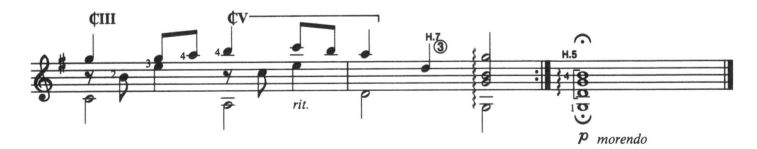

THE FIRST NOEL

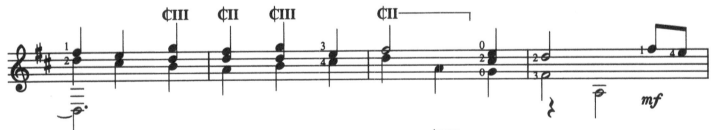

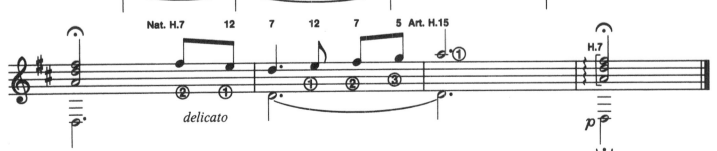

IT CAME UPON THE MIDNIGHT CLEAR

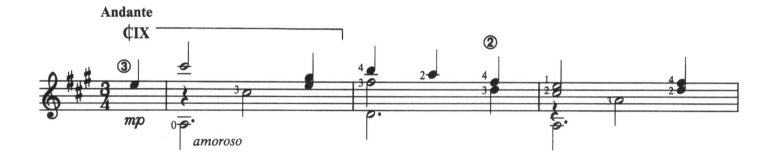

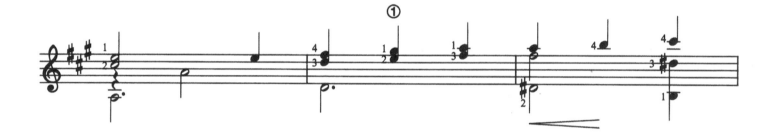

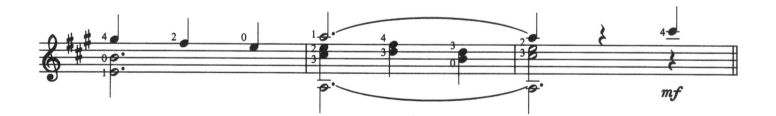

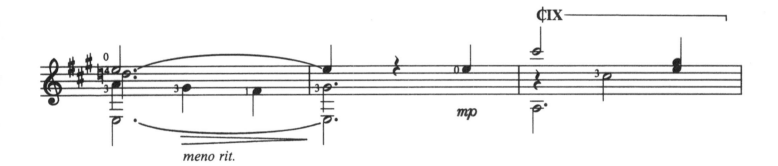

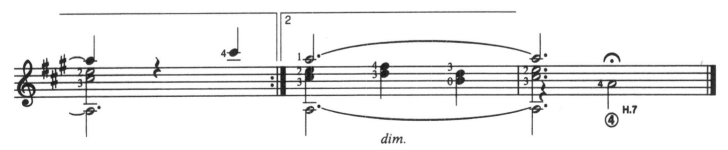

O HOLY NIGHT

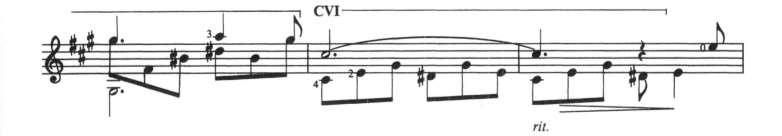

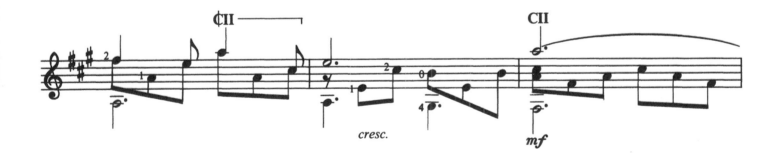

GOOD KING WENCESLAS

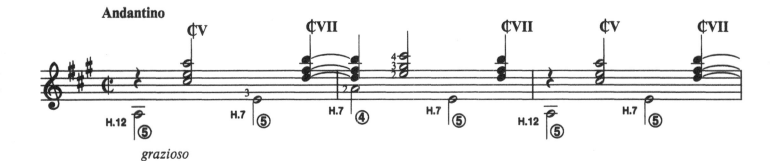

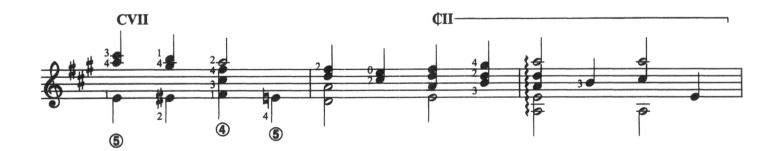

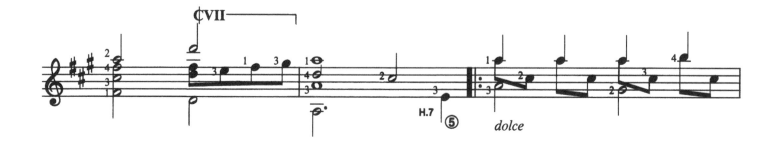

38

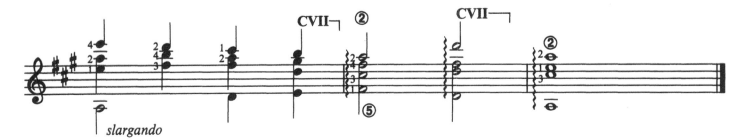

AWAY IN A MANGER

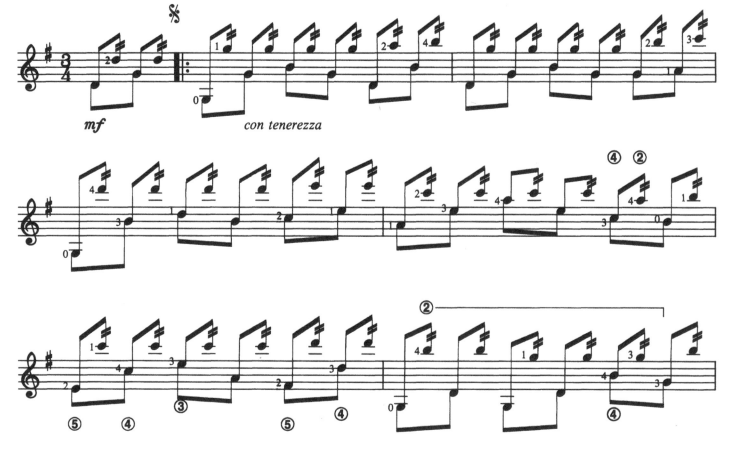

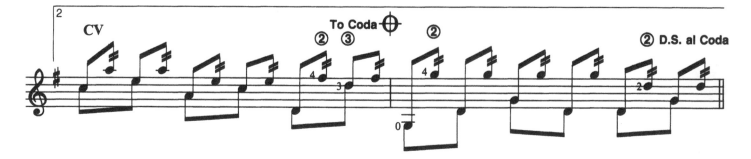

WE WISH YOU A MERRY CHRISTMAS

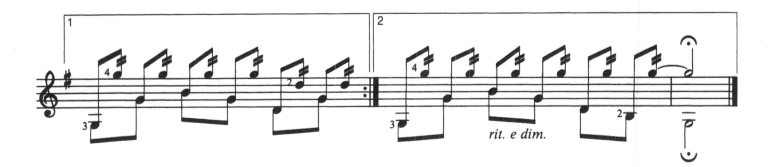

SILENT NIGHT

Amoroso

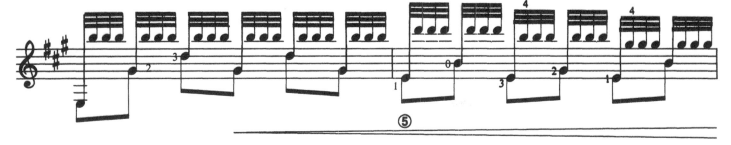

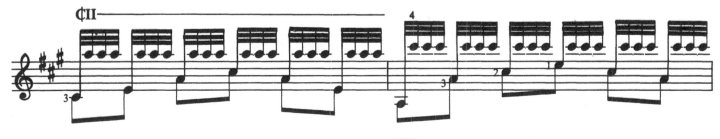

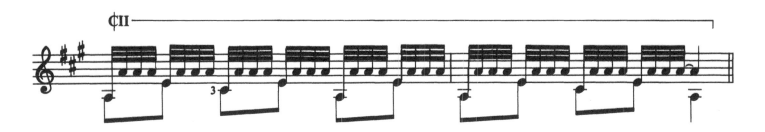

O COME ALL YE FAITHFUL

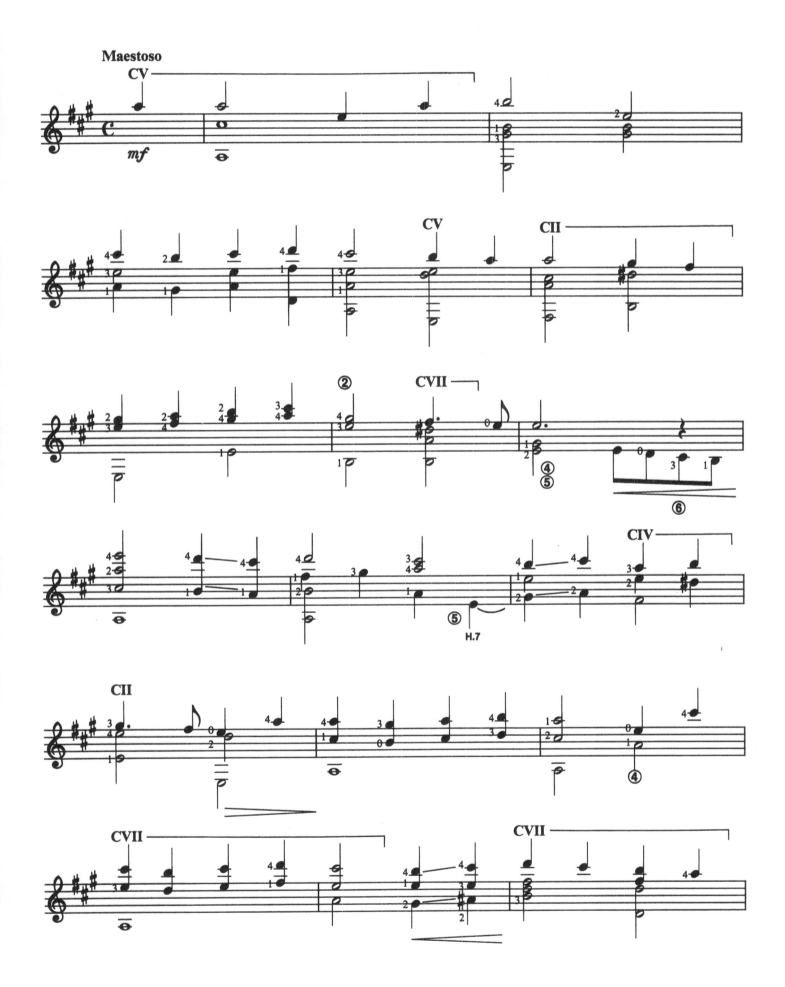

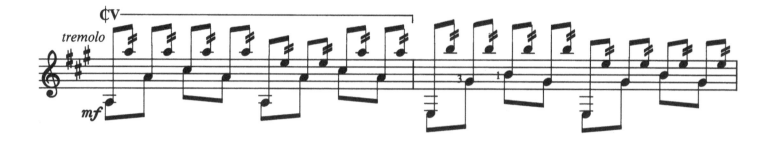

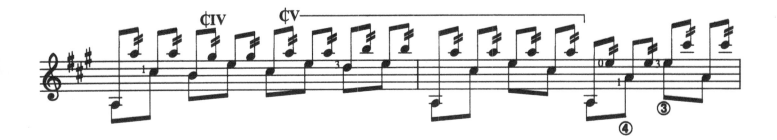

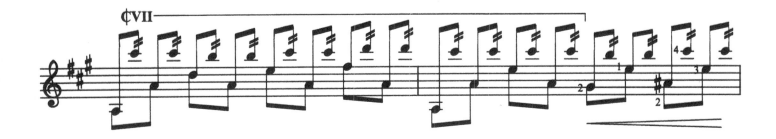

47